THE DEAD SEA
THE SALTIEST SEA

Aileen Weintraub

The Rosen Publishing Group's
PowerKids Press™
New York

Published in 2001 by The Rosen Publishing Group, Inc.
29 East 21st Street, New York, NY 10010

First Edition

Book Design: Michael de Guzman and Emily Muschinske
Illustrations on pp. 4 and 7: Emily Muschinske

Photo Credits: Background image on all pages, pp. 11, 12, 20, 22 and photo of archaeologist on p.16 © Richard T. Norwitz/CORBIS; p. 8 © Dave Houser/CORBIS; p. 14 © Archivo Iconagraphico, S.A./CORBIS; p. 15 © Jeffrey Rotman/CORBIS; p. 16 (fragment of Dead Sea Scroll only), p. 19 (scientists) © Nathan Benn/CORBIS; p. 19 (cave) © David Bartruff/FPG; p. 20 (inset) © Michael Philip Manheim/Stock Photo.

Weintraub, Aileen, 1973–
     The Dead Sea: the saltiest sea / Aileen Weintraub.
       p. cm.— (Great record breakers in nature)
     Includes index.
     Summary: Discusses the Dead Sea, describing the features that make it unique as well as the scrolls that were discovered in nearby caves.
     ISBN 0-8239-5637-7 (alk. paper)
     1. Dead Sea (Israel and Jordan)—Juvenile literature. [1. Dead Sea (Israel and Jordan) 2. Dead Sea Scrolls.] I. Title.
II. Series.

DS110.D38 W45 2000
956.94—dc21   00-023909

Manufactured in the United States of America

CONTENTS

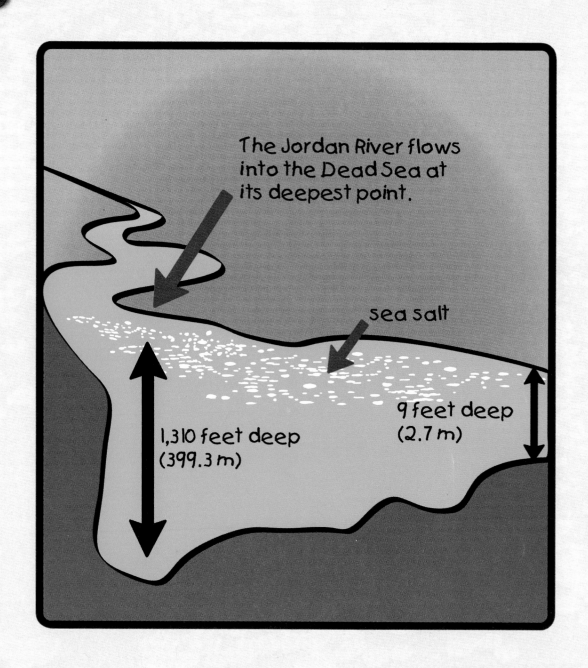

The Jordan River flows into the Dead Sea at its deepest point.

sea salt

1,310 feet deep (399.3 m)

9 feet deep (2.7 m)

4

THE SALTIEST SEA ON EARTH

Have you ever tasted ocean water while swimming in the ocean? It probably tasted pretty salty! Now imagine a sea that is seven times saltier than normal ocean water. The Dead Sea is the saltiest sea in the whole world. Its shoreline is also the lowest point on Earth's surface. The shoreline is where the sea meets the land. The Dead Sea's shoreline is 1,300 feet (396.2 m) below **sea level**. The Jordan River pours into the Dead Sea's northern end, where the water is deepest. This part of the sea is 1,310 feet (399.3 m) deep from the surface of the water to the sea floor.

◄ *The shallowest part of the Dead Sea is only 9 feet (2.7 m) deep.*

THE GREAT RIFT VALLEY

The Dead Sea is located in the Middle East on the continent of Asia. It lies between the countries of Israel and Jordan. The Dead Sea is in the Great **Rift** Valley, a deep valley that runs from southwest Asia to east Africa. In the Great Rift Valley, Earth's **crust** is being pulled in different directions. When this happens, Earth's surface sinks downward. Imagine pulling apart a piece of chewing gum. As you stretch it, the middle gets thinner and thinner. Earth's crust beneath the Dead Sea is like a piece of chewing gum. The Dead Sea sinks almost 13 inches (33 cm) per year. That may not seem like a lot, but over hundreds of years it can make a huge difference in the level of the Dead Sea.

The Dead Sea is the lowest point in the world because Earth's crust keeps sinking in this area.

The Dead Sea is in the Rift
Valley. A Valley is a low
area between mountains.

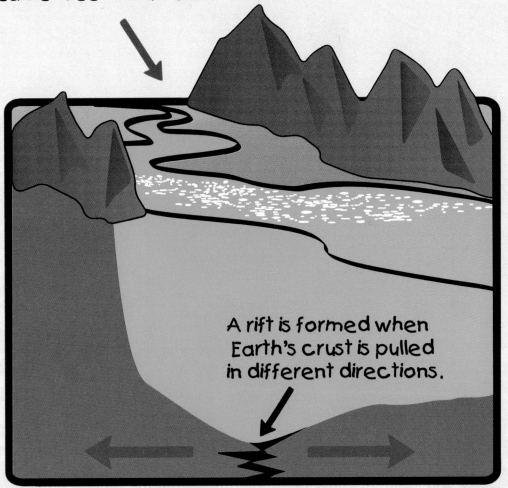

A rift is formed when
Earth's crust is pulled
in different directions.

WHERE DOES ALL THAT SALT COME FROM ANYWAY?

The Dead Sea covers 394 square miles (1,020 sq km). It is 46 miles (74 km) long and 10 miles (16 km) wide. Mountains surround the Dead Sea. Water flowing down the mountains collects salt **minerals** from soil and rocks. Even though the Jordan River flows into the Dead Sea, there are no rivers that drain out of it. The only place the water can go is up into the air. This is called **evaporation**. The Dead Sea is in a hot, desert **environment**. This makes the water evaporate quickly. About 55 inches (139.7 cm) of water disappear from the Dead Sea each year. When the water evaporates, the salt and minerals are left behind. This is why the Dead Sea is so salty.

The Dead Sea contains 12.7 billion tons (12.9 billion tonnes) of salt. When the water evaporates, all that salt is left behind.

THE CLIMATE BY THE DEAD SEA

The area around the Dead Sea has an unusual **climate.** It is hot, dry, and hazy. Water evaporates so fast that there is hardly any moisture in the air. The area has very high temperatures and little rainfall.

There is a special layer in the air around the Dead Sea. This layer of the **atmosphere** comes from the evaporating water and the minerals in the sea. The layer acts like a natural sunscreen. It blocks the sun's harmful rays. The air around the Dead Sea is also one of the most **oxygen-**rich places on Earth. It has up to eight percent more oxygen than most air at sea level.

Towers, or mounds, of salt form in the Dead Sea.

12

HOW THE DEAD SEA GOT ITS NAME

The Dead Sea is so salty that almost nothing can survive in its water. This is why it is called the Dead Sea. Fish that accidentally swim from the Jordan River into the Dead Sea die immediately. They become coated with a layer of salt and then get tossed ashore by the wind and waves. Plants and seaweed can't live in the Dead Sea either. Recently scientists have found different types of **bacteria** and **algae** living in the Dead Sea. The bacteria are so tiny that you can't see them without special equipment. Scientists use **microscopes** to study the bacteria. They are trying to figure out how the bacteria and algae can survive in the salty Dead Sea water.

◀ *Hardly any living things can survive in the Dead Sea's very salty water.*

PEOPLE AND THE DEAD SEA

Even though plants and animals can't live in the Dead Sea, that doesn't keep humans away. Humans are very **adaptable**. They can spend time in the Dead Sea without being hurt by all that salt. A lot of people enjoy going to the area around the Dead Sea. The air is very clean and healthy. There are beautiful mountains to hike and many old caves to explore. It is even believed that ancient cities once existed nearby. Two of these cities were Sodom and Gomorrah, which are mentioned in the Bible. The Dead Sea has a long, interesting history full of mystery and excitement.

In this picture, a boy and his father enjoy the sun and the Dead Sea. ▶

◀ *This painting imagines how the cities of Sodom and Gomorrah looked as they were being destroyed by fire.*

FINDING THE DEAD SEA SCROLLS

In 1947, young Bedouin shepherds living near the Dead Sea were searching for a goat that had run away. Like most Bedouin peoples, they lived in desert areas and moved from one area to another. The young shepherds entered a cave and found clay jars filled with ancient **scrolls** made from animal skin. The scrolls had writing on them. People around the world wanted to know more about this amazing discovery. This started a 10-year search for more scrolls. Soon, thousands of pieces of scrolls were found in 11 different caves near the Dead Sea. Scientists worked very hard to find out what the scrolls had to say.

◄ *A scientist uncovers a piece of the Dead Sea Scrolls. The scrolls were found in small pieces.*

17

WHAT SCIENTISTS DISCOVERED ABOUT THE SCROLLS

Through special testing, scientists found out that the Dead Sea Scrolls were 2,300 years old. Scientists found stories written on the scrolls. Many of these stories were from the Bible. They were written in three different languages called Hebrew, Greek, and Aramaic. Many people still speak Hebrew and Greek. Aramaic is still spoken by a few people who live in small villages around the Dead Sea. These scrolls might have been part of a secret library. The scrolls may have been hidden in caves to protect them during wars that took place thousands of years ago. These scrolls remain one of the greatest discoveries of modern times.

The Dead Sea Scrolls were written in three languages called Hebrew, Greek, and Aramaic.

JUST FLOATING ALONG

The Dead Sea Scrolls have helped make the Dead Sea a very popular place to visit. People from all over the world come to float in the Dead Sea's special water. You're probably used to floating in the ocean with a life jacket. You need a life jacket in the ocean because you can drown if you're not careful. Well, would you believe that it is almost impossible to sink in the Dead Sea? All of that salt makes it very easy to float. You can't really swim in the Dead Sea because it is just too thick. It is easy to float in the Dead Sea, though, without even trying. All you have to do is lie on your back.

◄ *These people are floating in the Dead Sea without much effort. The man is even reading a book!*

FAMOUS MUD

Since ancient times, mud from the Dead Sea has been used for many different things. The mud is rich in minerals. The minerals in the Dead Sea are thought to have many healing and cleansing properties. People collect the mud and put it on their bodies to make their skin feel soft and smooth. Ancient Romans used the mud to help heal the war wounds of injured soldiers. Humans have benefited from the Dead Sea for centuries. The saltiest sea in the world is one of the most fascinating places on Earth.

Today mud from the Dead Sea is used to make soap and shampoos and is sold around the world. ▶

GLOSSARY

adaptable (uh-DAP-tuh-bul) When someone or something is able to change with different conditions.

algae (AL-jee) Plants without roots or stems that live in the water.

atmosphere (AT-muh-sfeer) The layer of gases that surround an object in space. On Earth, this layer is air.

bacteria (bak-TEER-ee-uh) Tiny living things that can only be seen with a microscope and sometimes cause illness.

climate (KLY-mit) The kind of weather a certain area has.

crust (KRUST) The top, outer layer of Earth.

evaporation (ih-va-puh-RAY-shun) When moisture is removed from a liquid and it changes to a gas.

environment (en-VY-urn-ment) All the living things and conditions that make up a place.

microscopes (MY-kruh-skohps) Instruments used by scientists to help them see things that are too small to see otherwise.

minerals (MIH-ner-ulz) Natural ingredients from Earth's soil that are not plants or animals.

oxygen (AHK-sih-jin) A gas in the air that has no color, taste, or odor, and is necessary for people and animals to breathe.

rift (RIFT) When plates break apart and make a crack in Earth's crust.

scrolls (SKROHLZ) Rolls of paper or animal skins used for writing.

sea level (SEE LEHV-ul) A way to measure how high or low something is on Earth's surface.

INDEX

WEB SITES

To learn more about the Dead Sea, check out these Web Sites:
http://www.centuryone.com/25dssfacts.html
http://www.mrdowling.com/607-deadsea.html

24